Love &
Restlessness and All
That's In- Between

Darah Macaraeg

BookLeaf
Publishing

India | USA | UK

Presentation by *BookLeaf Publishing*

Web: www.bookleafpub.com

E-mail: info@bookleafpub.com

ISBN: 9789360945596

First edition 2024

To my parents, Rachel and Dante, and sister, Sarah for giving me the space and time to create without question.

ACKNOWLEDGEMENT

Thank you, God, for giving me the gift of writing in different forms. They give life to my imagination.

<u>Readers/Proofreaders</u>
Anna Marie Troupe, thank you for your time and support in reading my work, and listening to my stories. If I become a stand-up comedienne, I'll give you credit for being the first person to encourage it, if I have a successful career. :D

Leigh Anne Jones, you're a wonderful person. Thank you for your time and attention. I hope we get lost in discussing literature, and our own works in the future.

Kate Larot, thank you for reading my poems, and overall being a beautiful friend.

Cle Long, thank you for showing interest and reading my work. I look forward to many discussions about poetry.

<u>Places</u>
One House Bakery
Benicia, CA
Thank you for making one my favorites, the lavender oat latte. I appreciate the upstairs area where some of the pieces were created.

Benicia Library
Benicia, CA
My go-to library with a fireplace. Thank you for being open on Sundays.

The Chill - Benicia Wine Bar
Benicia, CA
I love your intimate space. The first time I came to the wine bar, I wrote a poem there inspired by the space and patrons while sipping on Segura Viudas Sparkling Rose. I'll be back. :)

Springstowne Library
Vallejo, CA
Thank you for existing in my neighborhood. I borrowed poetry books to jolt my creative poetic juices. This is where I worked my first job.

<u>Special Shout Outs</u>
San Francisco State University
Thank you to the Creative Writing department
where I honed in my skills as a playwright and
poet. I earned my BA and MA in Creative
Writing and minored in Asian American Studies.

Solano Community College
Fairfield, CA
I'm happy that I started my journey here as a
young adult. I learned to become confident and
figured out what I wanted to do: write, create
and be outspoken. I'm blessed to be on the other
side serving students.

PREFACE

With this challenge of writing a poem a day, I wondered where the process would mentally take me. I dedicated a specific time each day to be still, quiet and gather my thoughts. Such an exercise was beneficial for me because it made me put away my phone and practice mindfulness. This opened up wounds, and subconsciously, I revisited certain buried memories. I followed the challenge strictly by crafting a poem each day. This means each poem was made with raw emotion. Some pieces were about what happened that day and others about what happened years before. I wrote about exes, insomnia, writer's block, being tired of work, aging, meeting a new love interest and being alone. For each written word, I was honest and vulnerable because deep down inside I wanted to heal and recover and move forward. At the end, I realized I've done so much of the work already.

I hope each piece will evoke an emotion or memory in the kindest way encouraging the reader to be the writer.

Darah Ramos Macaraeg
Vallejo, California
April 2024

Moment

Our hands intertwined
Causing
My heart to wander in endless possibilities
My mind tries to
    undermine
        this emotional euphoria

Lying next to you feels nice
So easily I can be enticed
    into a fantasy driven
by the warmth of your body,
your hand on my thigh,
and our legs on top of one another like branches.

This is only a moment.
Savor its sweetness.

Tomorrow comes with
no commitment,
no future
no good morning or good night.

But tomorrow is not here
It has not yet arrived
For now, our hands remain intertwined.

Lies

"He's not as fine as you think."
My brain thinks it can outweigh
my heart with its logic.
My heart is blind
      as it confides
to anyone who wants to hear.

               To bear
such delusions
   or intrusions into what
should/could
be a
productive day.

Instead the heart entertains such foolishness.

Effects of Caffeine Are Amazing

A sip from a cup of cappuccino
    from a local cafe
    does wonders for my
    drooping eyelids.

At a library,
focusing on words and
making sense of them
are
the most difficult things
when all I want to do is sleep on the
book's pages.

Every few seconds,
    I nod off.
My hand supporting
    this heavy head
    is an
impromptu pillow
    that can only do so much
    as this is
NOT
    its
primary purpose.

I am tempted
   to lay my head on
   this library's table, but
   this will bring me
neck pain and a
   bitchy attitude.

I could go home and nap.
But my history dictates that
I will fail to reach immediate slumber
and
I will likely
stare and scroll
endlessly on my phone.
This will give me a
bitchy attitude.

Solution is
going to a cafe,
sipping
on a cappuccino
at a cafe
among other
caffeine addicts
while they converse amongst each other.

This wakes me up,

makes me energized to rigorously write words on paper.

Insomniac

I prefer to stay up all night
when no one
in my household is in sight.

While I sit at my desk
at the far corner of the house,
I'm like a mouse, secretive and
quiet,
But instead of nibbling away at a piece of fallen
bread,
I'm obsessing to finish reading a novel
Or
Writing any worries to rid myself of endless
evening rumination.

Back to Love When the Stingers Fall off

I lost at love twice.
Is third time the real charm?
Will it do more harm?

Will it sting me deeper than the last,
    piercing my skin
with its fangs,
venom almost killing me,
just enough to paralyze
and wake me
and jolt me
…simultaneously.

Reminder:
Should you love again?
Should you put yourself out there…
…after you healed
            reflected
            prayed
            exercised
            prayed again
            forgiven
                    him
                    you

me
you
him
me
us?

The grasslands and swamps of
            snakes
    will make themselves known
        in my new found lens.
Wide—rimmed, they're clean with no scuffs, no
marks

Yes, love is a back and forth,
a type of dance that we choose to…
        …swing
    …sway
    …swerve
    …curve
    …manuever
    …undo
    …redo
    …make do
    …come through
    …pull
        and push through.

Love is a fine thread
trying to find the eye of the needle.

Observance

Walk vigorously onto a path that's unfamiliar.
Birds hop from branch to twig to trunk and
ground.
Lost in thought.
Be in this moment
of nature.
Forget what is left and move on to what's ahead.
Earth is the trusted foundation.
Observe to stay in control.
Nothing else is important other than what is
seen.
Beauty is the tree that swiftly sways in the
breeze.
Quick is the squirrel that zips on the grass.
Happiness is walking and waking up to cool air.
Being well is existing.

Flying Straight Ahead

Give me wings!
Don't tell me where to go!
Allow me to cut through clouds.
Soar above steep mountains and terrain.
I'll go my way and you'll find yours.
The winds may cross our paths again.
If they don't, it was nice walking around with
you.
Weren't we walking around in circles in the end?

Conversation

The Girl:
Tell me about the man you used to love.

The Woman:
Why would you ask about the shiniest star that
died and fell out of the night sky?

The Girl:
I want to know what heart break feels like.

The Woman:
Love is your own type of journey.
You start with someone or someone starts with
you.
You blindly accept temptation's offers,
question the last turn you made,
try to turn back,
but it's too late because you're committed.

You are a warrior after all.

You decide to keep going, then it gets darker
and
now you're way
into deep into

who knows what.

You have seen and said things you wish to
remove from memory.

Turning back is not an option.

You move forward to start over,
to shed a part of you that you once knew
and at that same time gain a new,
unrecognizable you.

The Girl:
I don't want to fall in love.

The Woman:
Good answer.

What I Want

I want to write the meaningful words
that have occupied my brain
day in and day out.

I have a hard time articulating.

I stare at the mug filled with pens —clickers and
with tops,
and pencils — shaven, unshaven, and
mechanical
as if gazing at them they will tell me how to
capture my thoughts.

Nearby sits an intentional lidless jar filled
with colored pencils waiting to be used
for the next coloring book excursion.

I want to open my mind and write
fluidly and beautifully like a conductor tracing
and jabbing the air,
orchestrating melodic sounds out of instruments
that make the audience weep triggering
melancholy memories or past joys.

For now, I sit alone in my room,

thoughts fly like butterflies looking for a place
to land.
They dance in the air.
I watch for a moment,
hoping to capture each one to examine,
assess,
learn,
note down and let go

Birthday

A milestone age is ahead.
I'm about to make that turn.
I refuse to reach it.
Make the anti-aging elixir for me to drink it
daily
because death quickly approaches.

It is morbid.

Everyone will go sometime.
I hope to be surrounded by loved ones.
Five people and a dog will suffice.

I attended a funeral.
I cried for the deceased.
I cried harder from the reaper's reminder of our
mortality.

Attraction Can Kill

Often wonder why I was attracted to you.
Like a fly to an electric zapper.

Yet I wanted to be close to you.
You're wonderfully unappealing
when I speak to you.
Humor non-existent,
Love is both blind and deaf.

For a few moments, we kept each other
company.
Sparks fly when we touch,
That's all we had,
Not enough to make anything last

Birthday Notice

Ex's birthday is in five days.
I'm quickly saddened by this reminder.
A saved calendar event on my phone from years
ago.
I deleted it.
I'm sorry.
Part of me still grieves.
We shared something beautiful
like a rose before it wilted.
We kept it alive as long as we could.
Naivety made us blind.
We realized this rose was clipped with garden
shears.

Eventually, we picked up its wilted petals and
buried them.
If we opened our eyes a lot wider, would we
have tried to keep going?
We held that last petal tightly until it was time to
let go.

At a Garage

The
be bold,
be unafraid,
don't give a shit mentality
was not in the forefront of my cerebral cortex
at 11am on this particular Friday.

If the following happened:

Single?
I would have hurriedly written my phone
number
on a scrap of paper from my purse.

Taken?
I assisted a stranger rebuild his self-esteem
and
gave him a story to tell to his significant other.

Tall, dark and handsome
did not instantaneously register.
When he approached me, I feared for my life.

A quiet garage,
where there was no other human being in sight,

was the best setting for a jump scare.

From behind, he said, "Excuse me."
I turned quickly,
 felt my hands balled into fists.
"You scared me," I exclaimed.
He apologized.

He asked about the hotel's parking system.
His sophisticated accent
and
a deep voice grabbed my attention.

I fumbled with words like I had never spoken
before.
Ironically, he was in attendance for the
California Speech Language Hearing
Association Conference.
May I be your pupil?

Eventually, I regained the ability to form
sentences
and explained how parking worked.

He said, "Thank you" and left.

Hours later, from the comfort of my bed,
snuggled between blankets,
where there were no threats,

I came up with the brilliant idea
that I should have given him my number..

This bold act would have been ideal in real time.
Will I be able to identify such opportunities in
the future?

Smiling Man

One day,
riding on a MUNI train,
we stood next to each other, closely
in front of the doors,
in a packed car.
Rush hour.

All seats were occupied.

We didn't mind.

We amused ourselves --
laughed at silly things,
made weird voices,
and recalled cringeworthy moments.

This was what happiness felt like,
an exclusive world meant for both of us.
An old man
seated a few rows away,
smiled in our direction.

I didn't think anything of it.

At one of the stops,

he made his way to the doors to exit.
As we stepped aside
to let him pass,
he looked at us,
"You in love."
He smiled.
We were elated.
This was true then.

Since then, we stopped riding the train together.
I left the city.

Where is this man?
What would he say about us now?
Would he give us advice?
Would he console us?
Tell us that love is vicious as it is wonderful.
I would have agreed with him.
Love is like an ax.
It's sharp and swift
and
if you're not careful,
you may be severed.

The old man would nod his head
and
shed a tear.

Pursuit

Lately,

quite often,

in the evening,

when the clock turns from 10 to 11,
the only sounds I hear are coming from the
street,
speeding cars with screeching tires driving to or
away from their homes,
probably the latter.

We are all running away from something.

I'm in my room,

safe,

lost in thought

almost turning forty, scares me.
Losing the ability to have children.

cycle after cycle.
This is the only time I would love to be in my
early thirties.
Not any younger because I lacked experience
then.

Ironic,
I am a lot smarter,
wiser now,
make better income,
but my body is
                not getting younger.

We can't have everything.

Softly,
he rejected me because he wants babies.
I'm okay.
Spark was non-existent.
So the blow was not significant.

Or was it?
At first, it felt like a nudge, but slowly,
with more thought, it was feeling more like a gut
punch
slightly grazing my heart.

In the past,
I was weak then. I am sorry. I wasn't ready.

What does it mean to be happy?
With or without children?
Joy is found in both.
So...
What am I truly seeking?

Don't Give

It's okay to feel shitty,
defeated
and
have a don't-give-a-fuck attitude by the end of
the day.

The world is tiring
with its
endless
debilitating
issues.

Leaving me restless,
a tired recluse with
my limbs ready to fall off my body.
The weight on my shoulders is overbearing.

Remember,
I love the world,
I want peace, end all wars
and
include all the
typical beauty pageant answers ever stated,
but I'm human.

I keep going.
I am a soldier with a
soul of steel.
But I get rusty at times and need repair.
Spray me with WD-40, and
send me
to the nearest therapist.

Usually,
I'm a happy-go-lucky-
let's-conquer-the-world-
for-the-better type of woman warrior.

Lately,
my
energy has been drained
from
working,
walking up and down
the hallways of my building,
Zooming in and out of
online meetings, and
strategizing how to
shift and shape
the world into a
better state of well-being.

It's okay to admit fatigue
and tap out from

an eight-hour marathon that we all call work.

Because
tomorrow,
I am
renewed,
rejuvenated,
refreshed with ideas that I'll put into action.

But today,
at this moment,
I'm tired and
I don't give a fuck.

Alone Time

I'm having alone time among strangers.
I hear the chatter of wine lovers
after a long day
of who knows
what they do for a living
or not a living.

Who works in an office
or in the comfort of their homes?

Freedom to shower during their lunch break
or take a thirty-minute nap
during a ten-minute break.

I wonder who is coupled
or single among friends.
I have an idea. The boisterous one
that is speaking loudly to the group,
but only

one

other friend

is paying attention.

I relate to that one.

Fascinated by friendships
that might turn into something more,
but meet devastation.
I want to see someone else's
disastrous results,
but not live my own.

Rubbernecking a car wreck is gratifying.
Rubbernecking is a potential car wreck.
Aren't we all living in our own wreckage?

I'm a driver passing by.
I'm observing and listening,
catching cadence,
assuming
and
consuming their stories,
note taking and interpreting.

Single life among strangers is satisfying.

Weekend

Saturday, walked to you in a packed cafe,
white wine and coffee on table.
Our conversation made me
wonder about you.
Striped shirt, flower clip.
Notebook, pen in hand.
Our energies were drawn to one another
like magnets finding
each other's vulnerability.
Next day, I hope to match.
Text and tell me you want to see me.

We have desires. Mine and yours will likely be
the same.

Sunday comes,
my email has your name,
give you a day to reach me.
At Church, I see God.
You say morning and I respond.
Electricity cuts through text. I want to keep
conversing,
but His presence is next. You'll have to wait.

We both have desires. Will we share the same?

Later, we continue,
text
to
test each other's compatibility
How do you figure in? I'm wondering.
I live in the moment, excited to know you,
want to see your smile again.
Next Sunday, I'll ask about your notebook.
My hair will have a different colored flower clip.

Stay Low

There is no need to fly me to the moon
when you would rather take me gliding among
the clouds.

I prefer this.

The bright, blue sky
as my backdrop brings me
back to earth when things are batshit crazy.

Too much space makes me lonely.

The sky gives me enough freedom.
I look down and remember where I'm from.
When I miss it, I'll come down again.

Don't have to go as high as you think to show
me who you are.
Stick to the ground as close as you can.
Say hello randomly, and
say my name exactly how I like it.
Listen, then do.
Life can go as high as you want it to be
when following instructions.

Breeze

Right now, I'm steady.
I feel the cool breeze.
My hair surfs through the wind.
I close my eyes, pretend I'm flying.
For once, I'm released from all worries

I want to feel this always.
Bottle it, and carry it with me.
Drink it when I need a fix.

I'm usually constantly moving, not swiftly, but
erratically,
finding my way, through the thicket, cutting
blurred lines.

Yet, I'm fortunate to find the flashlight.

Life is a whirlwind.
Strap me onto a kite so I can fly high.
Caught in the breeze.
Again, I'm released from all worries.